Table of Contents

Introduction

The names Double Pinwheel and Double Windmill both describe this traditional pattern. A pattern called Double Windmill was published by the Old Chelsea Station Needlecraft Service, a mail-order company begun in 1933. The company is still in business today, although most of their quilt patterns are no longer offered.

You will find Double Pinwheel a most enjoyable quilting experience. The surprise is turning out an equal number of pinwheels that spin in different directions. One set of pinwheels is for the body of the quilt and the other set is for the border. The center of the pinwheel appears to be made from four pieced squares, but you don't make pieced squares in this easy method!

You'll enjoy this quilt particularly because it isn't necessary to "square up" the blocks! If you cut the strips carefully and sew a consistent seam allowance, the blocks will just "spin" together.

My first playmate to spin pinwheels for me was my sister Kathy. We were good playmates growing up together, always twisting and turning in the same direction. Sisterhood is as a set of strong blades, that even great winds cannot blow away. Even though we live far apart, our lives still spin together.

May making this quilt be child's play for you!

Eleanor Burns

Planning Your Quilt

The Block

Yardages are provided for both Small and Large Block quilts in each size from Wallhanging to King. Four quarters make up one block. Large Block quilts are easier and faster because there are fewer blocks. However, the smaller size blocks are more traditional looking.

This strip method produces two kinds of pinwheels, or mirror image pinwheels. You automatically have blocks for the body of the quilt and blocks for the border. The body and border pinwheels turn, or spin, in different directions so they may not be used together. In the Three Fabric and Multi-fabric quilts, the colors are reversed in the two blocks.

Small Block, Three Fabric
Approximately 7" finished size

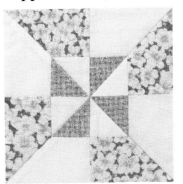

Large Block, Multi-fabric
Approximately 11" finished size

Number of Fabrics

The yardage charts give you the choice of making the Double Pinwheel quilt for either size block with Two Fabrics, Three Fabrics, or Multi-fabrics. The more contrast in the values, the more the pinwheel will show.

Two Fabrics

Choose two fabrics that have contrast, either in value or color. Call them Background and Dark. The effect is most dramatic when the two fabrics both read as a solid from a distance. Pinwheels using a Dark fabric of large prints, or different values and colors, are less distinct.

Teresa Varnes

The pinwheels for the body of the quilt and the pinwheels for the border look very much alike, but they turn in opposite directions.

Quilt Block *Border Block*

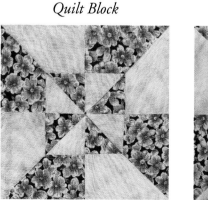

Blocks are mirror image.

Three Fabrics

Choose three fabrics that have contrast, either in value or color. Call them Background, Medium, and Dark. The effect is most dramatic when the Medium and Dark fabrics read solid from a distance. If your fabrics have large prints or if they have lots of different values or colors, the pinwheels are less distinct.

Trish Kuncewicz

The pinwheels for the body of the quilt and the pinwheels for the border look quite different. They turn opposite directions, but they also are generally Medium or Dark. You will need to decide if you want your quilt body to appear mostly Medium, or mostly Dark. Your border becomes the remaining value.

Quilt Block

Border Block

Dark forms inner pinwheel.
Block appears Medium.

Medium forms inner pinwheel.
Block appears Dark.

Multi-fabrics

Choose one Background Fabric, and a variety of other fabrics. The variety of fabrics may be one value, or Similar Value, as a collection of reproduction 1930's fabrics. Or half of the variety fabrics may be Medium and half Dark equal to the Background fabric.

This is the perfect choice if you like a scrappy looking quilt. Purchase small yardage cuts for variety, or substitute strips from your stash. Fat eighths cut 9" x 22" and fat quarters cut 18" x 22" are also perfect, because half strips are used in the construction of the quilt.

Similar Value Scrappy

For a very scrappy quilt, each quarter of a block may be of different fabrics. The pinwheel is less defined with many fabrics, but you can showcase your favorites.

Julia Markovitz

Loretta Smith

Similar Value Planned

This is the perfect choice if you like a scrappy looking quilt with a bit of organization. Each block has one Background, with one or two Similar Value prints.

Small Blocks

Making planned blocks is easy to do with the Small Blocks because of the method of construction. Each block uses two half strips of Background, and two half strips of Similar Value.

Large Blocks

Making planned blocks for the Large Blocks requires more thought. Follow this method of construction to yield three identical blocks. Count out eight half strips of Background, four identical half strips of one fabric, and four identical half strips of a second fabric, all in a Similar Value. Keep the strips together in groups as you sew.

If you prefer to make each planned block different, cut two Background strips and two Similar Value fabrics all at 3½" x 28". However, this method of construction is not as economical as making three identical blocks.

Similar Value Scrappy

Choosing fabrics in similar color values will give your quilt the look of a Two Fabric quilt. Use fabrics in the same color family, or with a similar print. This quilt uses a selection of Oriental print fabrics from the same line for a very defined pattern. Pinks and blues are featured in many of the prints used, giving the quilt a definite color theme, although it still has a scrappy look.

Marty Halus

This quilt works better if you use a plain Background fabric with your multi-fabrics. It will look like a Two Fabric quilt when made with prints in the same value.

Quilt Block

Border Block

Similar values of multi-fabrics appear to be a Two Fabric Quilt from a distance.

Dark and Medium Planned

This is the perfect choice if you like a scrappy looking quilt with a definition in the pattern. Each block has one Background, with one Medium print and one Dark print.

Group your Multi-fabrics into Mediums and Darks with the help of a view finder. This quilt does take longer when selecting fabrics, combining Quarter Blocks, and arranging Blocks, but the end result is well worth it.

Small Blocks

Making planned blocks is easy to do because of the method of construction. Each block uses two half strips of Background, one half strip of Medium, and one half strip of Dark.

Large Blocks

Making planned blocks for the Large Blocks requires more thought. Follow this method of construction to yield three identical blocks: Sew eight half strips of Background with four identical half strips each of Medium and Dark. Keep strips together in groups as you sew.

If you prefer to make each planned block different, cut two Background strips, one Medium strip, and one Dark strip, all at 3½" x 28". This method of construction is not as economical as making three identical blocks.

Teresa Varnes

Quilt Block   *Border Block*

Mediums and Darks of multi-fabric appear to be a Three Fabric Quilt.

Pinwheel Borders

You automatically make the blocks for the border while you make blocks for the body of the quilt. The two blocks are equal in number. Since these two kinds of pinwheels turn different directions, do not mix the quilt blocks with those used for the border.

Background Border

The Background border that separates the body of the quilt from the pinwheel border is the same width as a Quarter block. This width allows the border to fit exactly with the body of the quilt.

Two Border Rows

There are enough Small Blocks for two border rows on the Queen and King quilts. If you want to enlarge these quilts with a second row of border blocks, be sure to increase the size of your batting and backing, and add more binding. These dimensions will increase by approximately 14".

Eleanor Burns

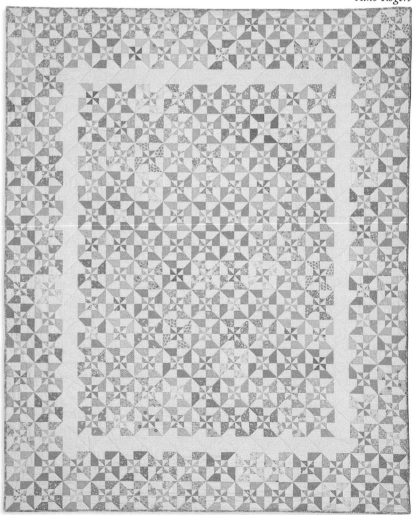

Aiko Rogers

Two Quilts instead of One

You may use the Border pinwheel blocks to make the body of a second quilt. This is particularly useful for making a pair of lap or twin size quilts. You'll have two similar quilts, but without pinwheel borders. If you want to use your blocks this way, you'll need to plan borders for both of them. This affects the binding, backing and batting yardages listed on the Yardage Chart.

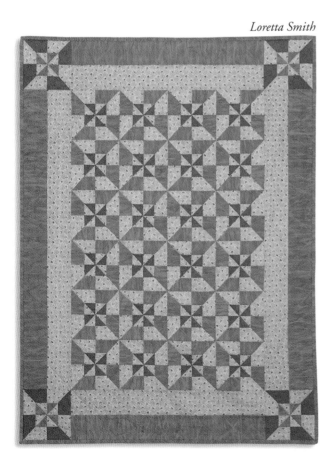

Loretta Smith

Loretta Smith

Border Options

You may customize the size of your quilt by changing the borders. This Three Fabric quilt has been enlarged by adding additional borders outside of the pinwheel border. Extra Border blocks finish the corners.

Linda Fornaca

You may also finish your larger quilt with the Half Block border used in the Small Block wallhanging on page 49. The pieced border is made so that the width equals a Quarter Block. By using Half Blocks in her border, the quiltmaker had enough Border Blocks left over to make a small companion quilt.

Vivien McNeece (both)

Paste-up Blocks

Blocks for the quilt body and the border are made automatically at the same time. However, the blocks can't be mixed, because they spin in different directions. Choose the block you will use for your Quilt Body and the block you will use for the Border.

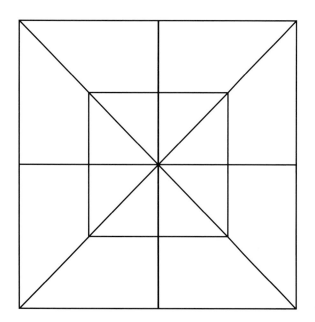 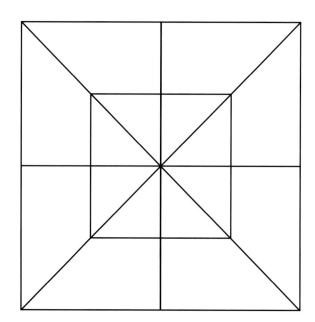

Two Fabric Blocks

Trace two patterns on paper side of fusible web. Cut 3" squares from your Background and Dark fabrics. Fuse patterns on wrong side of fabric. Cut on lines, and tear away paper. Fuse in place following sample blocks.

Three Fabric Blocks

Trace three patterns on paper side of fusible web. Cut 3" squares from your Background, Medium and Dark fabrics. Fuse patterns on wrong side of fabric. Cut on lines, and tear away paper. Fuse in place following sample blocks.

Supplies

Square rulers must have 45° diagonal lines marked corner to corner.

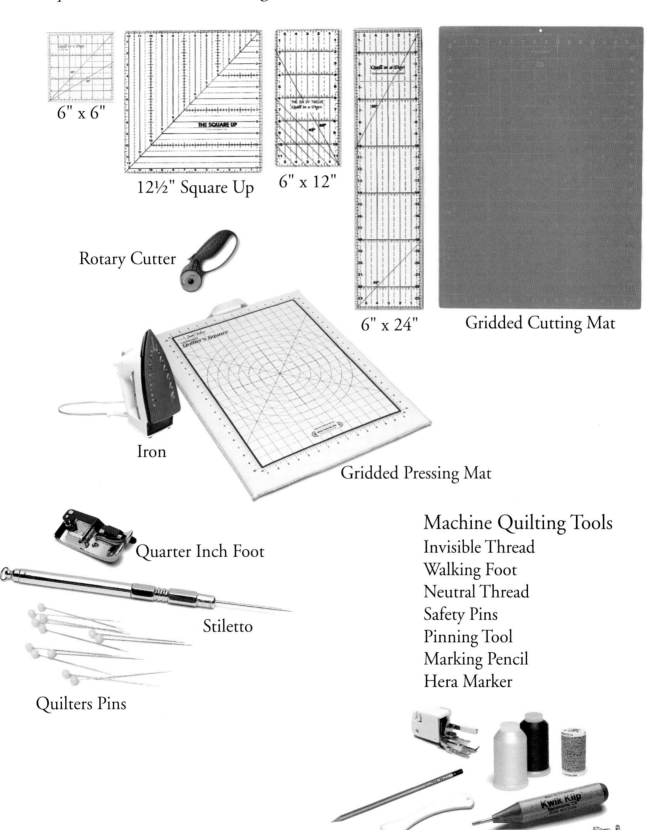

6" x 6"

12½" Square Up

6" x 12"

6" x 24"

Gridded Cutting Mat

Rotary Cutter

Iron

Gridded Pressing Mat

Quarter Inch Foot

Stiletto

Quilters Pins

Machine Quilting Tools
Invisible Thread
Walking Foot
Neutral Thread
Safety Pins
Pinning Tool
Marking Pencil
Hera Marker

Yardage Charts

Large Block Wallhanging

4 Quilt Blocks
4 Border Blocks

2 x 2   44" x 44"

	Background	Medium	Dark	Backing	Batting
Two Fabric	1½ yds Cut (6) 3½" strips Cut 4 border strips later		2 yds Cut (6) 3½" strips Cut (5) 3" binding strips Cut (4) border strips later	50" x 50" or 3 yds total	50" x 50"
Three Fabric	1½ yds Cut (6) 3½" strips Cut 4 border strips later	½ yd Cut (3) 3½" strips	1⅔ yds Cut (3) 3½" strips Cut (5) 3" binding strips Cut (4) border strips later	50" x 50" or 3 yds total	50" x 50"
Multi-Fabric	1½ yds Cut (6) 3½" strips Cut 4 border strips later	(6) ⅛ yds **similar value** Cut (1) 3½" strip each for 6 total or (3) ⅛ yds Medium and Cut (1) 3½" strip each for 3 total	1¼ yds for binding and border Cut (5) 3" binding strips Cut (4) border strips later (3) ⅛ yds Dark Cut (1) 3½" strip each for 3 total	50" x 50" or 3 yds total	50" x 50"

Small Block Wallhanging

9 Quilt Blocks
16 Half Border Blocks
4 Quarter Blocks

Eleanor Burns

3 x 3   35" x 35"

	Background	Medium	Dark	Backing	Batting
Two Fabric	1⅓ yds Cut (10) 2½" strips Cut 4 border strips later		1¼ yds Cut (10) 2½" strips Cut (4) 3" binding strips	1¼ yds	43" x 43"
Three Fabric	1⅓ yds Cut (10) 2½" strips Cut 4 border strips later	½ yd Cut (5) 2½" strips	⅞ yd Cut (5) 2½" strips Cut (4) 3" binding strips	1¼ yds	43" x 43"
Multi- Fabric	1⅓ yds Cut (10) 2½" strips Cut 4 border strips later	(10) ⅛ yds **similar value** Cut (1) 2½" strip from each for 10 total or (5) ⅛ yds Medium and Cut (1) 2½" strip from each for 5 total	½ yd for binding Cut (4) 3" binding strips (5) ⅛ yds Dark Cut (1) 2½" strip from each for 5 total	1¼ yds	43" x 43"

Large Block Lap Robe

12 Quilt Blocks
22 Border Blocks

Peggy Kile

3 x 4

66" x 77"

	Background	Medium	Dark	Backing	Batting
Two Fabric	4½ yds Cut (30) 3½" strips Cut 6 border strips later		4 yds Cut (30) 3½" strips Cut (8) 3" binding strips	4⅔ yds	74" x 85"
Three Fabric	4½ yds Cut (30) 3½" strips Cut 6 border strips later	1¾ yds Cut (15) 3½" strips	2½ yds Cut (15) 3½" strips Cut (8) 3" binding strips	4⅔ yds	74" x 85"
Multi-Fabric	4½ yds Cut (30) 3½" strips Cut 6 border strips later	(30) ⅛ yds **similar values** Cut (1) 3½" strip each for 30 total or (15) ⅛ yds Medium and Cut (1) 3½" strip each for 15 total	¾ yds for binding Cut (8) 3" binding strips (15) ⅛ yds Dark Cut (1) 3½" strip each for 15 total	4⅔ yds	74" x 85"

Small Block Lap Robe

24 Quilt Blocks
28 Border Blocks

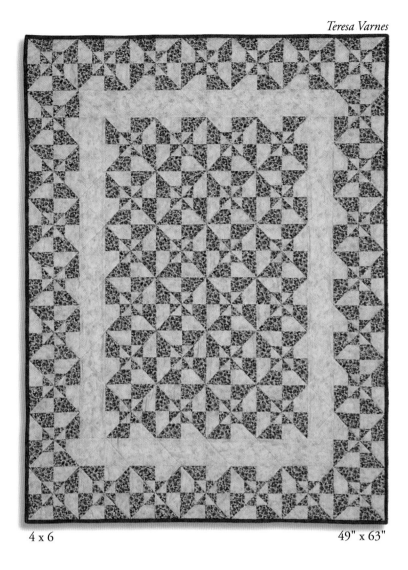

Teresa Varnes

4 x 6   49" x 63"

	Background	Medium	Dark	Backing	Batting
Two Fabric	3 yds Cut (28) 2½" strips Cut 5 border strips later		3 yds Cut (28) 2½" strips Cut (6) 3" binding strips	4 yds	57" x 71"
Three Fabric	3 yds Cut (28) 2½" strips Cut 5 border strips later	1¼ yds Cut (14) 2½" strips	2 yds Cut (14) 2½" strips Cut (6) 3" binding strips	4 yds	57" x 71"
Multi-Fabric	3 yds Cut (28) 2½" strips Cut 5 border strips later	(28) ⅛ yds **similar value** Cut (1) 2½" strip each for 28 total or (14) ⅛ yds Medium and Cut (1) 2½" strip each for 14 total	¾ yds for binding Cut (6) 3" binding strips (14) ⅛ yds Dark Cut (1) 2½" strip each for 14 total	4 yds	57" x 71"

Large Block Extra Long Twin

21 Quilt Blocks
28 Border Blocks

Sue Bouchard

3 x 7   66" x 110"

	Background	Medium	Dark	Backing	Batting
Two Fabric	5½ yds Cut (38) 3½" strips Cut 7 border strips later		5 yds Cut (38) 3½" strips Cut (8) 3" binding strips	6⅔ yds	74" x 118"
Three Fabric	5½ yds Cut (38) 3½" strips Cut 7 border strips later	2 yds Cut (19) 3½" strips	3 yds Cut (19) 3½" strips Cut (8) 3" binding strips	6⅔ yds	74" x 118"
Multi-Fabric	5½ yds Cut (38) 3½" strips Cut 7 border strips later	(38) ⅛ yds **similar value** Cut (1) 3½" strip each for 38 total or (19) ⅛ yds Medium and Cut (1) 3½" strip each for 19 total	1 yd for binding Cut (8) 3" binding strips (19) ⅛ yds Dark Cut (1) 3½" strip each for 19 total	6⅔ yds	74" x 118"

22

Small Block Twin

55 Quilt Blocks
40 Border Blocks

Teresa Varnes

5 x 11   56" x 98"

	Background	Medium	Dark	Backing	Batting
Two Fabric	5 yds Cut (55) 2½" strips Cut 7 border strips later		5 yds Cut (55) 2½" strips Cut (8) 3" binding strips	6 yds	64" x 108"
Three Fabric	5 yds Cut (56) 2½" strips Cut 7 border strips later	2¼ yds Cut (28) 2½" strips	3 yds Cut (28) 2½" strips Cut (8) 3" binding strips	6 yds	64" x 108"
Multi-Fabric	5 yds Cut (56) 2½" strips Cut 7 border strips later	(19) ¼ yds **similar value** Cut (3) 2½" strips each for 56 total or (10) ¼ yds Medium and Cut (3) 2½" strips each for 28 total	1 yd for binding Cut (8) 3" binding strips (10) ¼ yds Dark Cut (3) 2½" strips each for 28 total	6 yds	64" x 108"

Large Block Double/Queen

35 Blocks
32 Border Blocks

Laura McCauley

5 x 7   88" x 110"

	Background	Medium	Dark	Backing	Batting
Two Fabric	6½ yds Cut (48) 3½" strips Cut 8 border strips later		6 yds Cut (48) 3½" strips Cut (11) 3" binding strips	10 yds	96" x 118"
Three Fabric	6½ yds Cut (48) 3½" strips Cut 8 border strips later	2¾ yds Cut (24) 3½" strips	3½ yds Cut (24) 3½" strips Cut (11) 3" binding strips	10 yds	96" x 118"
Multi-Fabric	6½ yds Cut (48) 3½" strips Cut 8 border strips later	(48) ⅛ yds **similar value** Cut (1) 3½" strip each for 48 total or (24) ⅛ yds Medium and Cut (1) 3½" strip each for 24 total	1 yd for binding Cut (11) 3" binding strips (24) ⅛ yds Dark Cut (1) 3½" strip each for 24 total	10 yds	96" x 118"

Small Block Double/Queen

Aiko Rogers

108 Quilt Blocks
50 Border Blocks

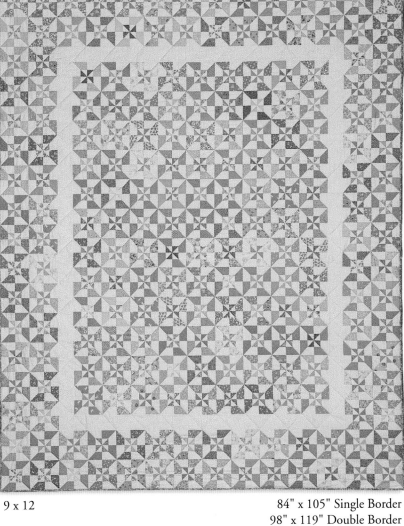

The Double/Queen has one row of Border Blocks. There are enough Border Blocks for a second row, if you would like a larger Queen quilt. If you choose to add this second Border row, purchase 11 yards for Backing, 120" x 132" for Batting, and an additional ¼" yard for Binding.

9 x 12

84" x 105" Single Border
98" x 119" Double Border

	Background	Medium	Dark	Backing	Batting
Two Fabric	8¾ yds Cut (108) 2½" strips Cut 8 border strips later		8¾ yds Cut (108) 2½" strips Cut (10) 3" binding strips	9¾ yds	96" x 120"
Three Fabric	8¾ yds Cut (108) 2½" strips Cut 8 border strips later	4¼ yds Cut (54) 2½" strips	5 yds Cut (54) 2½" strips Cut (10) 3" binding strips	9¾ yds	96" x 120"
Multi-Fabric	8¾ yds Cut (108) 2½" strips Cut 8 border strips later	(36) ¼ yds **similar value** Cut (3) 2½" strips each for 108 total or (18) ¼ yds Medium and Cut (3) 2½" strips each for 54 total	1 yd for binding Cut (10) 3" binding strips (18) ¼ yds Dark Cut (3) 2½" strips each for 54 total	9¾ yds	96" x 120"

25

Large Block King

49 Quilt Blocks
36 Border Blocks

Urbana Schneider

7 x 7

110" x 110"

	Background	Medium	Dark	Backing	Batting
Two Fabric	8½ yds Cut (66) 3½" strips Cut 9 border strips later		8 yds Cut (66) 3½" strips Cut (12) 3" binding strips	10 yds	120" x 120"
Three Fabric	8½ yds Cut (66) 3½" strips Cut 9 border strips later	3¾ yds Cut (33) 3½" strips	4¾ yds Cut (33) 3½" strips Cut (12) 3" binding strips	10 yds	120" x 120"
Multi Fabric	8½ yds Cut (66) 3½" strips Cut 9 border strips later	(66) ⅛ yds **similar value** Cut (1) 3½" strip each for 66 total or (33) ⅛ yds Medium and Cut (1) 3½" strip each for 33 total	1⅛ yds for binding Cut (12) 3" binding strips (33) ⅛ yds Dark Cut (1) 3½" strip each for 33 total	10 yds	120" x 120"

Small Block King

Luckie Yasukochi

144 Quilt Blocks
56 Border Blocks

12 x 12

105" x 105" Single Border
119" x 119" Double Border

There are enough Border Blocks for a second row, making the quilt approximately 14" larger and wider. If you choose to add this second Border row, purchase 11 yards for Backing, 132" x 132" for Batting, and an additional ¼ yard for Binding.

	Background	Medium	Dark	Backing	Batting
Two Fabric	11½ yds Cut (144) 2½" strips Cut 9 border strips later		11½ yds Cut (144) 2½" strips Cut (11) 3" binding strips	10 yds	120" x 120"
Three Fabric	11½ yds Cut (144) 2½" strips Cut 9 border strips later	5½ yds Cut (72) 2½" strips	6½ yds Cut (72) 2½" strips Cut (11) 3" binding strips	10 yds	120" x 120"
Multi Fabric	11½ yds Cut (144) 2½" strips Cut 9 border strips later	(48) ¼ yds **similar value** Cut (3) 2½" strips each for 144 total or (24) ¼ yds Medium and Cut (3) 2½" strips each for 72 total	1⅛ yds for binding Cut (11) 3" binding strips (24) ¼ yds Dark Cut (3) 2½" strips each for 72 total	10 yds	120" x 120"

27

Cutting Strips

Cut the number of strips listed on your yardage chart.

1. If your fabrics were cut from the bolt rather than torn, put them on grain by snipping a cut in the selvage at one end and tearing across to the other selvage. Skip this if you have ⅛ or ¼ yard pieces as you may lose too much.

2. Clip the selvages every few inches to relieve selvage tightness.

3. Lay a folded fabric on the cutting mat with the torn end beyond a grid line to the left and selvages across the bottom.

4. Place the 6" x 24" ruler and rotary cutter on the grid line and trim the left end.

5. Lift and reposition the ruler for your width strip. Use the mat's grid lines if they match your ruler lines.

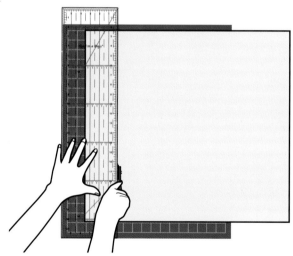

Large Block quilt
  Cut 3½" wide strips.

Small Block quilt
  Cut 2½" wide strips.

6. Consistently cut the same width strips. "Step stack" the strips for easy counting.

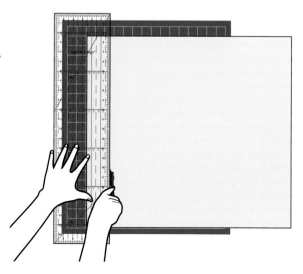

7. Count your strips of each fabric. Keep the stacks separate.

Two Fabrics quilt
- Dark strips equal to Background strips

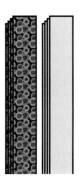

Three Fabrics quilt
- Dark and Medium equal to Background strips

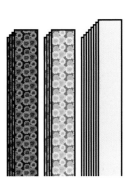

Multi-fabrics quilt
- similar value strips equal to Background strips
or
- Dark and Medium equal to Background strips

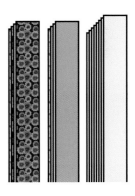

8. Cut each strip in half. Use the 6" ruler and rotary cutter to sliver trim the fold.

9. Stack the half strips of each fabric right side up with the selvages at the bottom.

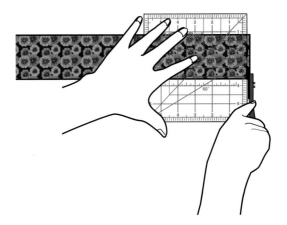

Sewing Strips

1. Set your machine to 15 stitches per inch, or a machine setting of 2.

2. Set a consistent seam width approximately ¼" wide. The seam does not have to be a perfect ¼", but it must be consistent. Use a guide such as a ¼" foot or a magnetic seam guide to assure a consistent and straight seam.

3. Lay out equal stacks of half strips with Background always on the right and selvage ends at the bottom. The selvage ends may be different lengths.

Two Fabrics quilt
   • Dark and Background

Three Fabrics quilt
   • Dark and Background
   • Medium and Background

Multi-fabrics quilt
   • Similar Value and Background
   or
   • Dark and Background
   • Medium and Background

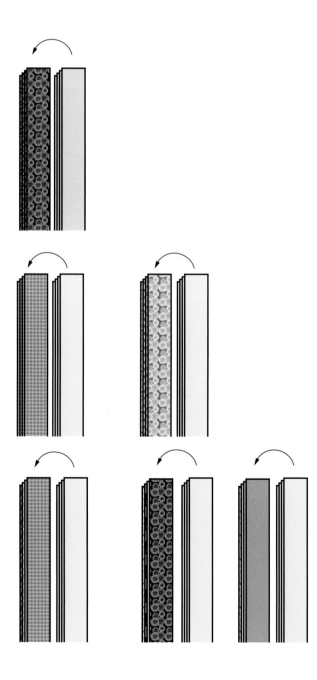

4. Flip the Background to the darker strip, right sides together matching the top end.

5. Assembly-line sew pairs by continuously sewing sets one after the other with a consistent ¼" seam.

6. Clip apart.

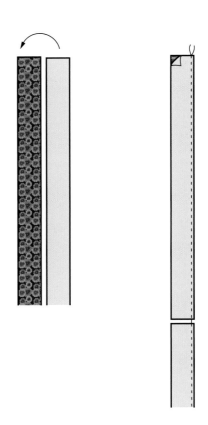

Pressing Sets of Strips

1. Lay out sewn pairs on a gridded pressing mat with the darker fabric on top and the Background fabric underneath. **It is important that the Background fabric is underneath.** Line up the strip with lines on the pressing mat.

2. Press the stitching to set the seam. Pressing with or without steam is your choice.

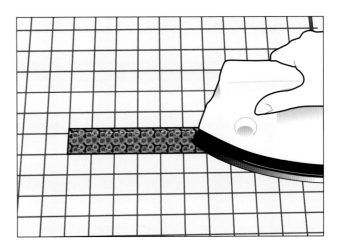

3. Open and press against the seams. The seams should lie behind the darker fabric.

4. **Keep Darks and Mediums in separate piles.**

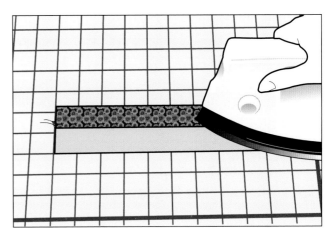

5. Arrange the sewn strips in pairs on the cutting mat, one set at a time. Place with Background across the top and selvages to the right.

Two Fabrics quilt
- two pressed open pairs
- Background fabric across top
- selvages at the right

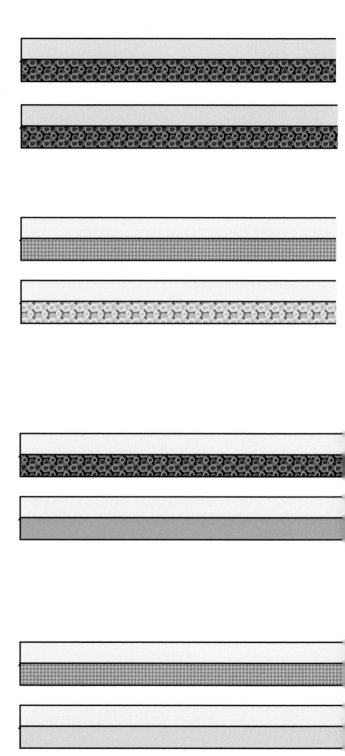

Three Fabrics quilt
- two pressed open pairs
- Background/Dark above Background/Medium
- Background fabric across top
- selvages at the right

Multi-fabrics quilt
- two pressed open pairs
- similar value fabrics that you want to appear together

or

- Background/Dark above a Background/Medium
- Background fabric across the top
- selvages at the right

6. Flip the upper pair down onto the lower pair, right sides together.

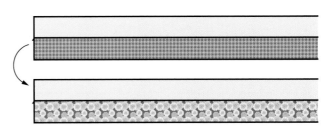

7. The Dark strip is now along the top. Run your fingers along the seams, and lock the seams together.

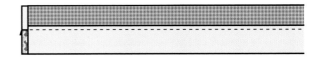

If outside edges do not line up, check to see if strips were cut at the correct width. You may be able to trim a wider strip.

8. **Optional:** Press with an iron.

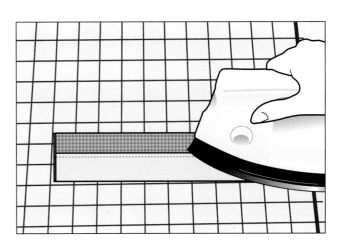

Making Quarters

Follow directions for Large Block on this page, or Small Block, next page.

Cutting Layered Squares for Large Blocks

1. Lay set of layered strips on a horizontal grid line of the cutting mat with left end beyond a grid line. **Place Dark strip across the top.**

2. Lay 12½" Square Up ruler on the left end grid line. Trim both layers, squaring off the end.

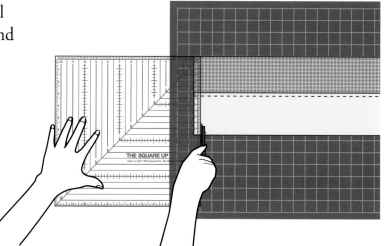

3. **Lay ruler on the top edge of the strips so that the ruler's diagonal line touches the left bottom end of the strips.** The diagonal line of the ruler confirms that you have measured a square. See the circles on the diagonal line.

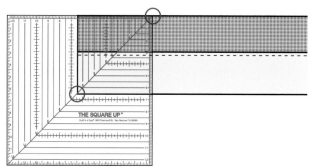

Large Block approximately 6½" square. Use diagonal line as your measurement.

4. Cut squares. You should get three squares across a set of strips.

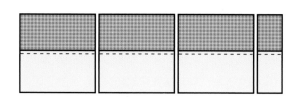

Cutting Layered Squares for Small Blocks

1. Lay set of layered strips on a horizontal grid line of the cutting mat with left end beyond a grid line. **Place Dark strip across the top.**

2. Lay 6" Square Up ruler on the left end grid line. Trim both layers, squaring off the end.

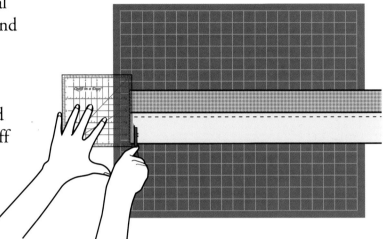

3. **Lay ruler on the top edge of the strips so that the ruler's diagonal line touches the left bottom end of the strips.** The diagonal line of the ruler confirms that you have measured a square. See the circles on the diagonal line.

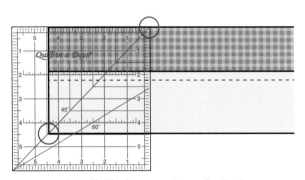

Small Block approximately 4½" square. Use diagonal line as your measurement.

4. Cut squares. You should get four squares across a set of strips.

5. **Optional:** Cut remainder of strip into 2½" section. Set aside and later sew into Bonus Four Patch Quilt, page 64.

Marking and Pinning Squares

1. Draw a pencil line diagonally across each square. It is important that the Dark strip is across the top and the pencil line runs from upper left dark corner to lower right Background corner. **Every square must be marked the same or you may have pinwheels turning several directions.**

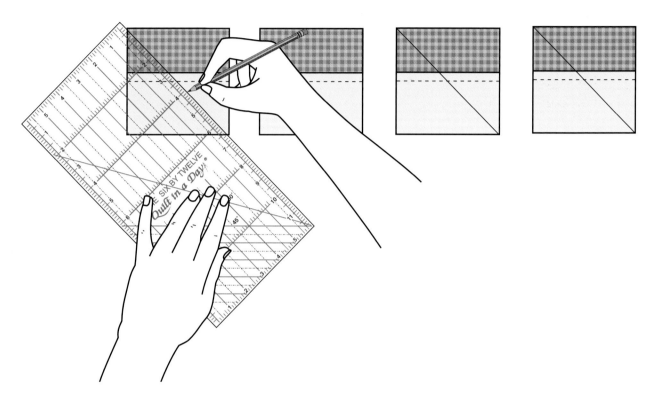

2. Pick up layered square and lock seams. Pin where seam and line meet.

3. Stack with Dark at the top.
   Multi-fabrics
   • Keep like Quarters together.

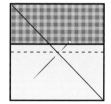

4. Cut, mark, pin, and stack this many layered squares:

	Large Block	Small Block
Wallhanging	16	36
Lap Robe	88	112
Twin	112	220
Double/Queen	140	432
King	196	576

Sewing Layered Squares

1. Assembly-line sew the pinned squares ¼"
   from the pencil line. Use a stiletto to feed
   squares and hold seams together.

   Sew a few at a time. It is important to sew
   an accurate and consistent ¼" distance
   from the line. Keep the layers locked and
   the edges together. Remove the pins as
   you come to them.

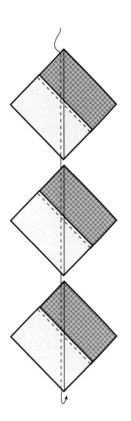

2. Turn the chain around and assembly-line
   sew ¼" from the pencil line.

3. Clip the chain of squares apart.
   Multi-fabrics
   • Keep like Quarters together.

4. Press the squares to restore the shape and
   to set the seams.

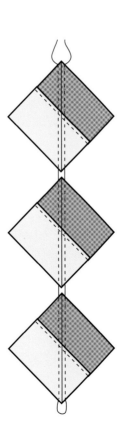

Cutting and Pressing Open Squares

1. Lay out square with **Dark across the top.**

2. Lay 6" x 12" ruler on the pencil line. Rotary cut on the pencil line, cutting the square into two pieces.

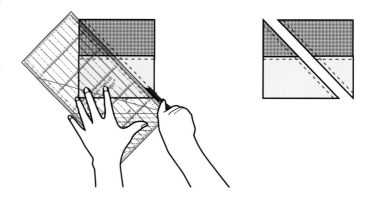

3. Carefully stack in two separate piles. Always place small triangles to the left. **Do not mix.** The two pieces of the square are used in the two different blocks, one for the quilt body, and one for the border. Each side forms a different "pinwheel."

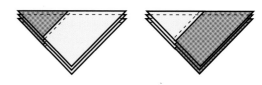

Do not mix stacks.

4. Separate out left stack. **Count out four pieces from stack.**

5. Trim tips at an angle to the stitching line. Use either a rotary cutter or scissors.

6. Place the trimmed pieces on a pressing mat, **with seam across the top.**

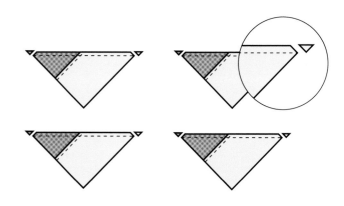

7. Lift open and gently press toward the seam, pushing the seam allowances to the upper triangle.

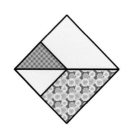

8. These squares are Quarters of one pinwheel block. Lay out block. Turn point of little pinwheel to center.

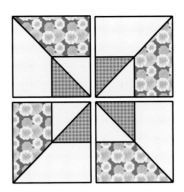

9. **Count out four pieces from right stack.** Trim tips at an angle to the stitching line.

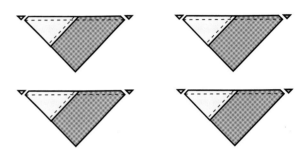

10. Place the trimmed pieces on a pressing mat, **with seam across the top.**

11. Lift open and gently press toward the seam, pushing the seam allowances to the upper triangle.

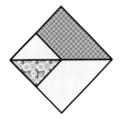

12. These squares are Quarters of second pinwheel block. Lay out block. Turn points of little pinwheel toward center.

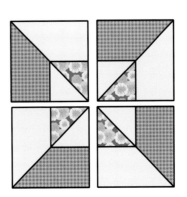

Choosing Quarters for Quilt Blocks

1. Decide which will be the Quilt Blocks and which will be the Border Blocks. This is more important for the Three Fabrics quilt than for the Two Fabrics quilt.

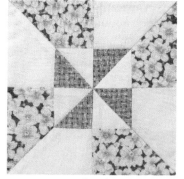 

Quilt Block   *or*   *Border Block*

2. Put aside the pieces for the Border. Work with them after making the blocks for the quilt.

3. Trim tips for selected Quarters.

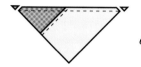 *or*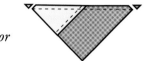

4. Gently press open the Quarters for the Quilt Blocks. Be careful not to distort the shape.

5. Place a square ruler on your Quarter to determine if it is square. If not square, try tugging gently at both ends of the stitching to pull it back in shape.

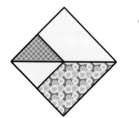 *or*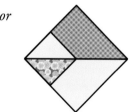

6. Measure and record the average size of your Quarters. Measure to the nearest ⅛". Use this size when cutting the width of your Background Border.

Size of your Quarter: _____"

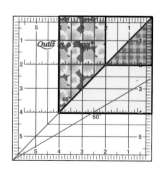

Making Quilt Blocks

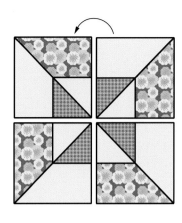

1. Be sure no Border Quarters are in the stacks. (Your block may be the mirror image of this illustration.)

2. Lay out equal stacks of Quarters to form the block. The number of Quarters in each stack is the number of blocks for your size quilt.

Multi-fabric Quilt Options

• Stack one block at a time so all Quarters are different for a scrappy look.

• Make four Quarters the same for a planned look.

	Large Block	Small Block
Wallhanging	4	9
Lap Robe	12	24
Twin	21	55
Double/Queen	35	108
King	49	144

3. Flip the Quarters right sides together.

4. Pin or wiggle-match the seams.

5. Assembly-line sew stacks. Leave a gap between blocks for easy separating.

6. Clip apart at the gap between blocks.

7. Stack the pairs of joined Quarters.

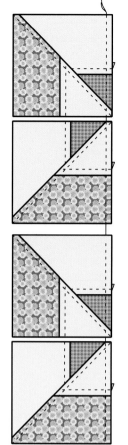

Clip apart.

8. Open and flip the pairs of Quarters right side together. **Push the top seam upward and underneath seam downward.** Wiggle-match or pin to match the center seams.

9. Assembly-line sew the blocks.

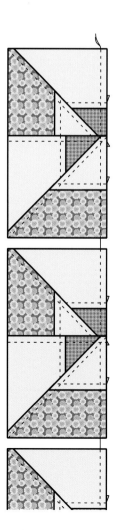

10. At the center seam, cut the first stitch with scissors. See circle. Remove the two or three straight stitches at the center on both sides with stiletto or seam ripper.

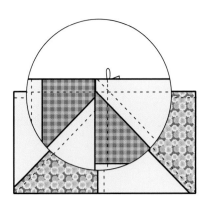

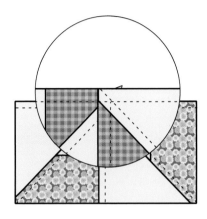

11. Open the center seams and push down flat to form a tiny pinwheel.

12. Press the seams clockwise around the block.

13. You may "sliver trim" to square them consistently, but it is not necessary if they are all close in size.

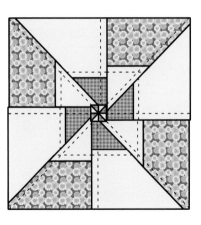

Depending on which block you choose, yours may spin differently or have a different value in the center.

Sewing the Blocks Together

1. Lay out the blocks according to your size quilt. See pages 46 and 47.

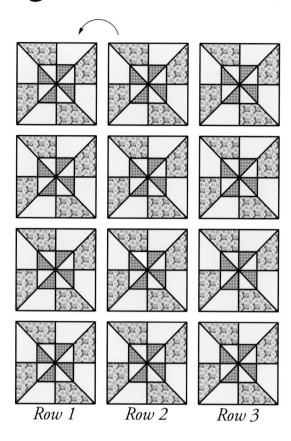

Row 1   *Row 2*   *Row 3*

2. Flip Row Two to Row One. Pin or wiggle-match and lock the seams. Stack and assembly-line sew.

3. Stack Row Three.

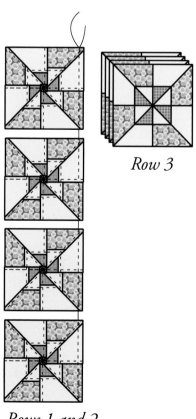

Row 3

Rows 1 and 2

4. Open Row One/Two, flip Row Three right sides together, and assembly-line sew.

5. Repeat for your number of rows across.

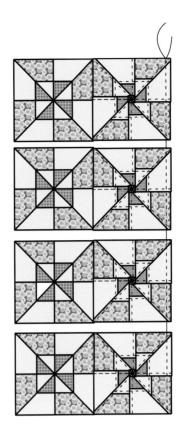

6. Flip the horizontal rows together. To avoid twisting the seams, lock and pin the seams. Push the seams between blocks in opposite directions.

7. Sew the remaining rows, consistently locking the seams and pushing the seams between blocks in opposite directions by row.

8. Press the quilt first on the wrong side, then on the right side.

9. If necessary, straighten the outside edges without removing ¼" seam allowances.

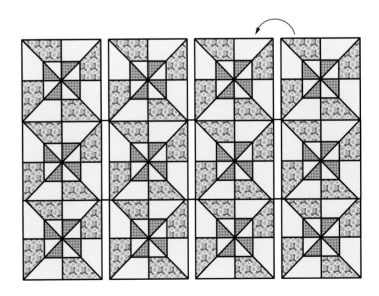

Large Block Layouts

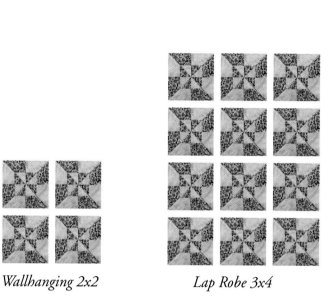

Wallhanging 2x2

Lap Robe 3x4

Extra Long Twin 3x7

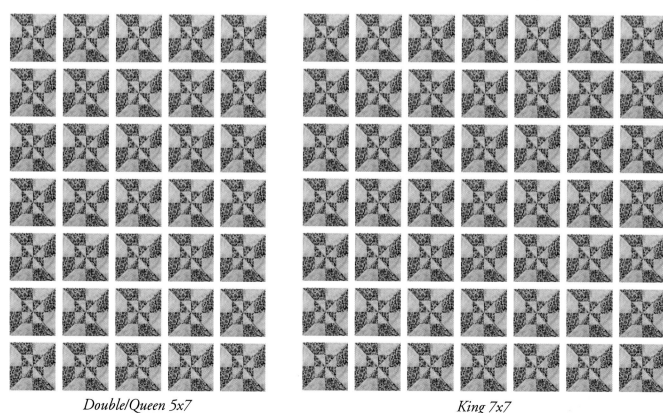

Double/Queen 5x7

King 7x7

Small Block Layouts

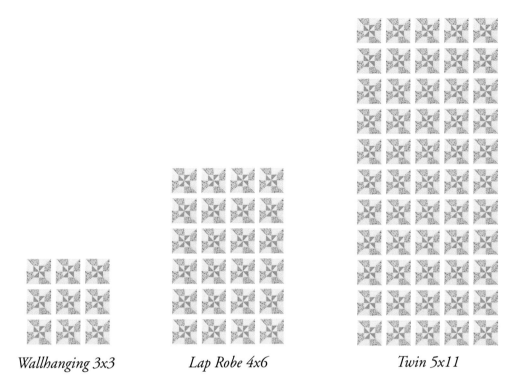

Wallhanging 3x3

Lap Robe 4x6

Twin 5x11

Double/Queen 9x12

King 12x12

Finishing Large Block Wallhanging

1. Cut four strips each from Background and Dark same width as Quarter Block. Refer to your measurement on page 40.

2. Sew Borders together with a ¼" seam. Press seams toward Dark.

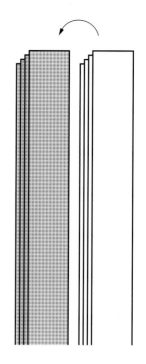

3. Sew four Border Blocks together.

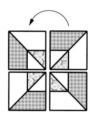

4. Cut four Border strips same length as quilt top.

5. Pin and sew Borders to two sides of quilt top.

6. Sew Border Blocks to ends of two remaining Borders. Pin and sew to quilt top.

7. Turn to page 58 for finishing.

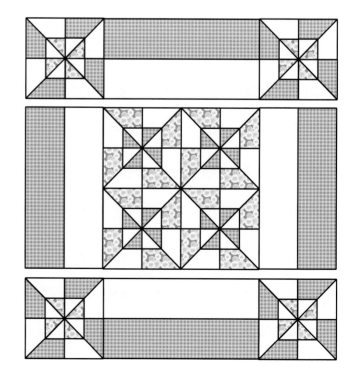

48

Finishing Small Block Wallhanging

1. Cut and sew Background borders to the top. See page 50 for instructions. (Your blocks may be mirror image of the illustrations.)

2. Place Quarters around outside of quilt.

   Planned Multi-Fabric
   - Carefully plan corners. Make a Half Block and set aside a matching Quarter Block for each corner.

3. Count out two piles of sixteen Quarter blocks. Assembly-line sew into sixteen Half Blocks.

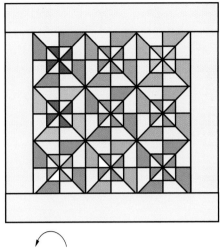

4. **Two sides:** Sew two sets of three Half Blocks together for sides. Sew a Quarter Block to each end.

5. Press seams in directions pieces will be sewn to top.

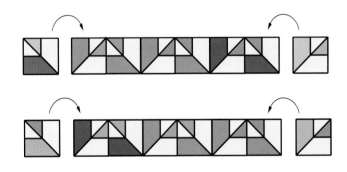

6. Pin and sew to quilt with patchwork on top. Press seams toward Background Border.

7. **Top and bottom:** Sew two sets of five Half Blocks together.

8. Pin and sew to quilt. Press seams toward Background Border.

Adding the Background Border

You may choose to have Square Corners on your Background Borders, or Mitered Borders.

1. The Background border is the same width as the Quarter so that the Border Blocks fit. Use the earlier recorded size of your Quarter measurement, page 40.

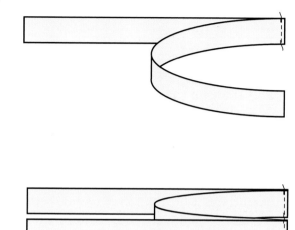

2. Cut the Background border strips listed on your Yardage and Cutting Chart. You may need fewer strips depending on the width of your Background fabric. For mitered corners, cut one additional strip.

3. Sew together, if necessary.

Making Square Corners

1. Measure the length of the quilt. Cut Background border strips for the left and right sides about 2" longer than the length.

2. Pin and sew the side borders to the quilt.

3. Press the seam allowances to the border.

4. Trim the ends even.

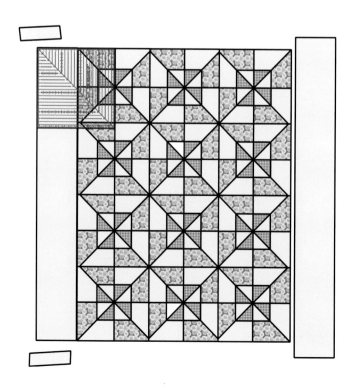

5. Measure the width of the quilt with side borders. Cut the top and bottom Background borders about 2" longer.

6. Pin and sew the top and bottom borders to the quilt.

7. Press the seam allowances to the border.

8. Trim the ends even.

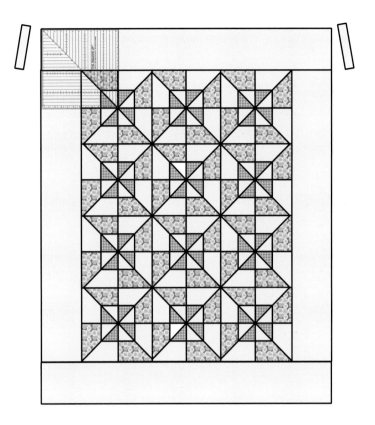

Mitered Corners on Background Border

1. Measure the length of the quilt. Add the length of Quarters plus 2" for each end. Cut Background Border strips for the left and right sides.

2. Center and pin borders on two opposite sides of quilt. Border should extend equally at each end. Along seam allowance, mark a dot at each end, ¼" in from edge.

3. Sew between the marked dots, and back-stitch at each end.

4. Press seams away from border.

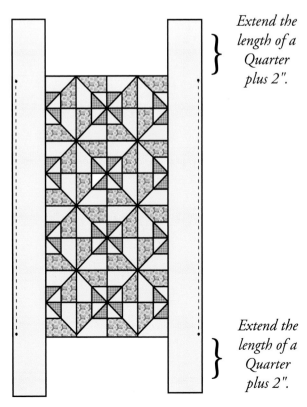

Extend the length of a Quarter plus 2".

Extend the length of a Quarter plus 2".

5. Measure the width of the quilt. Add the length of Quarters plus 2" for each end. Cut Background Border strips for the top and bottom.

6. Add two remaining borders, meeting in corners ¼" from edge.

7. To miter, place corner on pressing mat. Fold top strip under diagonally, and line up the two border strips. Press diagonal crease with iron.

8. Place Square Up ruler's 45° line on seam. Check that corner is square.

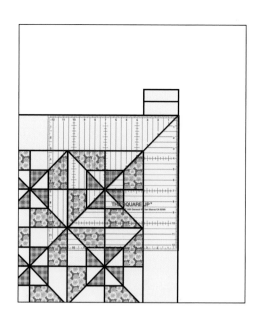

9. **Finishing Option One:** Pin in place. Sew from right side with blind hem stitch and invisible thread, straight stitch, or hand stitch.

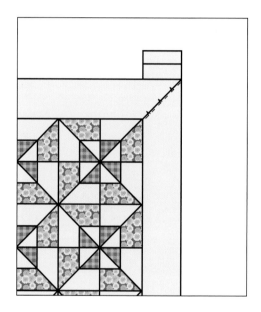

10. **Finishing Option Two:** Open wrong side up. Pin through the lines at the crease, lining up the two strips. Sew along the diagonal crease starting at ¼" dot. Trim seam allowance and press open.

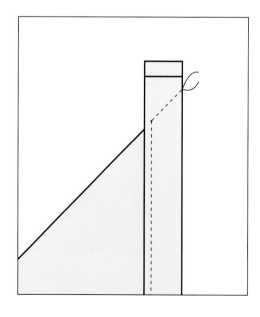

Making the Block Border

Solid Border Option

If you prefer solid borders or if you want a second quilt, you may use your border blocks for an entire new quilt the same size. The pinwheels will turn the opposite direction. You will need additional border yardage for both quilts, and additional yardage for the second's binding, backing and batting.

Small Block King and Queen Quilts

The King and Queen Small Block quilts have enough border pieces to make a double row of Border Blocks. If you enlarge these quilts with the additional row of Border Blocks, plan your backing, batting, and binding accordingly.

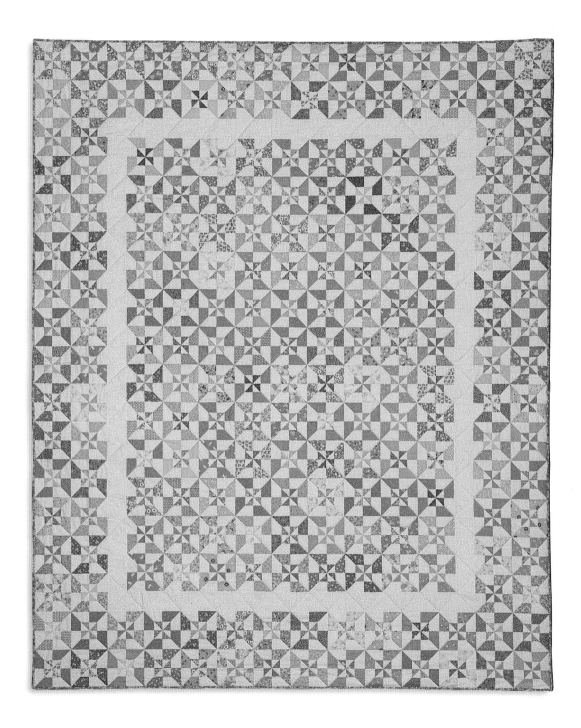

Making the Border Blocks

1. Use the stack of Quarters put aside for the Block Border.

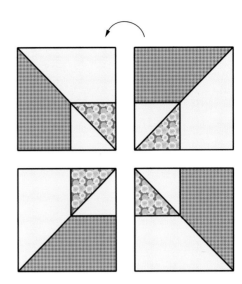

2. Trim the tips and press open the Quarters as you did with the one test square.

3. Lay out equal stacks of Quarters to form the block. The number of Quarters in each stack is the number of Border Blocks for your size quilt.

	Large Block	Small Block
Lap Robe	22	28
Twin	28	40
Double/Queen	32	50
King	36	56

Multi-fabrics quilt
- Stack one block at a time. Make all Quarters same in one Block or all Quarters different for a scrappy look.

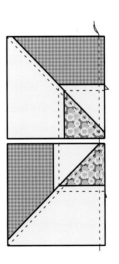

4. Assembly-line sew as many blocks required for your quilt.

5. Open the center seams and push down flat to form a tiny pinwheel.

6. Press the seams clockwise around the block.

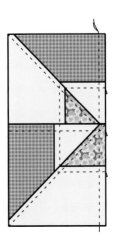

Adding Block Borders to Left and Right Sides

The width of two Background borders equals one block.

1. Count out Border Blocks for each side. Make two equal stacks.

2. Assembly-line sew Border Blocks for the left and right sides.

3. Pin and sew the side Border Blocks to the quilt. If Borders do not fit, make adjustments in seam allowances, or trim Background strip.

4. Press the seams to the Background border.

	Large Block	Small Block
Lap Robe	5	7
Twin	8	12
Double/Queen	8	13
King	8	13

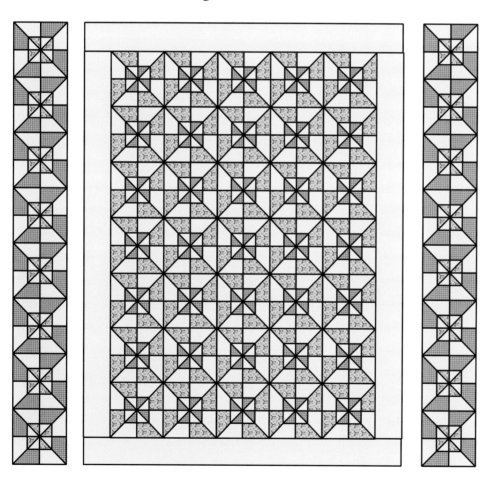

Adding Block Borders to Top and Bottom

1. Count out Border Blocks for top and bottom. Make two equal stacks.

2. Assembly-line sew Border Blocks together.

3. Pin and sew top and bottom Border Blocks to the quilt. If Borders do not fit, make adjustments in seam allowances, or trim Background strips.

4. Press the seams to the Background border.

5. Press the quilt top on the wrong side and then on the right side.

	Large Block	Small Block
Lap Robe	6	7
Twin	7	8
Double/Queen	8	12
King	10	15

Finishing the Quilt

Preparing the Backing

1. If your quilt is wider than your backing fabric, cut the backing yardage in pieces that are several inches longer than the quilt.

2. Clip the selvages every few inches to relieve selvage tightness.

3. Sew the backing pieces together to make a backing larger than the quilt.

Layering the Quilt

1. Spread out the backing on a large table or floor area with the right side down. Clamp the fabric to the edge of the table with quilt clips or tape the backing to the floor. Do not stretch the backing.

2. Layer the batting on top of the backing, and pat flat.

3. With the quilt top right side up, center on the backing. Smooth until all layers are flat. Clamp or tape outside edges.

Marking the Quilt

1. Using a Quilters Pencil, lightly pencil diagonal quilting lines across the Background border following the diagonal seams of the blocks. Quilters Pencils come in a variety of colors to accommodate almost any fabric color.

   You may also use a Hera marker. The Hera marker is a plastic tool with a sharp edge that is used to press in the lines to be sewn. It is held in much the same way as a rotary cutter with a ruler. Line up the marker with the ruler and push the tool away from you. The marker creases the fabric as you push, leaving a non-permanent line.

2. Mark diagonal lines in the other direction.

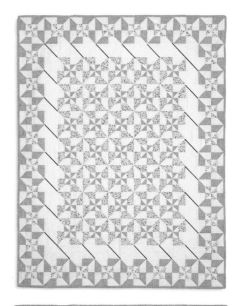

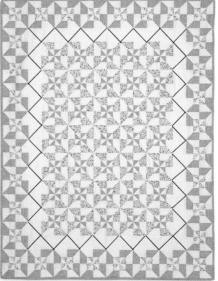

Pinning the Quilt

Safety pin the layers together every three to five inches. Use a pinning tool, the Kwik Klip™, to assist the process. Grasp the opened pin in your right hand and the Kwik Klip™ in your left hand. Push the pin through the three layers, take a ½" bite, and bring the tip of the pin back out. Catch the tip in the groove of the Kwik Klip™. Push pin closed. Pin next to your machine quilting lines.

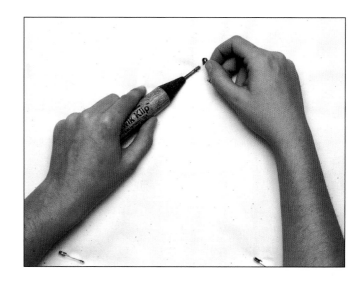

Machine Quilting

The ideal machine quilting area is a sewing machine bed level with the table, and a large area to the left of the machine to support the quilt. Machine quilt on a day when you are relaxed to help avoid muscle strain down your neck, shoulders, and back. Sit in a raised stenographer's chair so your arms can rest on the table.

"Stitch in the Ditch" to Anchor the Blocks and Borders

1. Thread your machine with matching thread or invisible thread. If you use invisible thread, loosen your top tension. Match the bobbin thread to the backing.

2. Attach your walking foot, and lengthen the stitch to 8 to 10 stitches per inch or 3.5 on computerized machines.

3. Roll on the diagonal to the center. Clip the rolls in place.

4. Spread the seams open, and "stitch in the ditch."

5. Unroll the quilt to the next diagonal seam. Clip the roll in place, and "stitch in the ditch."

6. Continue to unroll and roll the quilt until all the seams are stitched, anchoring the blocks.

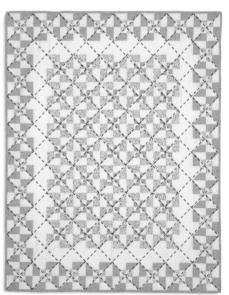

Adding the Binding

Use a walking foot attachment and regular thread on top and in the bobbin to match the binding.

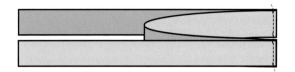

1. Square off the selvage edges, and sew 3" strips together lengthwise.

2. Fold and press in half with wrong sides together.

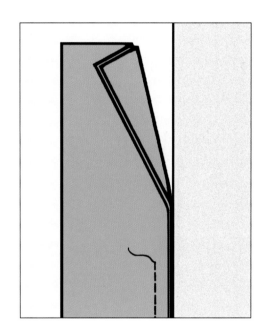

3. Line up the raw edges of the folded binding with the raw edges of the quilt in the middle of one side.

4. Begin stitching 4" from the end of the binding. Sew with 10 stitches per inch, or 3.0 to 3.5.

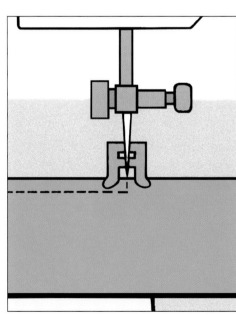

5. At the corner, stop the stitching ¼" from the edge with the needle in the fabric. Raise the presser foot and turn the quilt to the next side. Put the foot back down.

6. Stitch backwards ¼" to the edge of the binding, raise the foot, and pull the quilt forward slightly.

7. Fold the binding strip straight up on the diagonal. Fingerpress the diagonal fold.

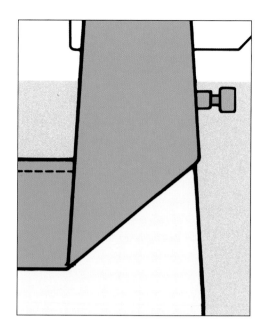

8. Fold the binding strip straight down with the diagonal fold underneath. Line up the top of the fold with the raw edge of the binding underneath.

9. Begin sewing from the edge.

10. Continue stitching and mitering the corners around the outside of the quilt.

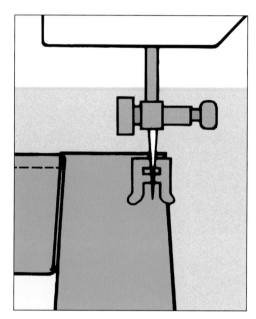

11. Stop stitching 4" from where the ends will overlap.

12. Line up the two ends of binding. Trim the excess with a ½" overlap.

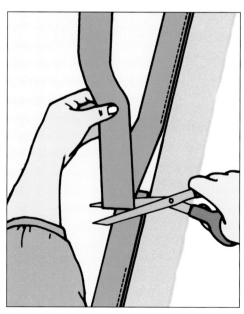

13. Open out the folded ends and pin right sides together. Sew a ¼" seam.

14. Continue to stitch the binding in place.

15. Trim the batting and backing up to the raw edges of the binding.

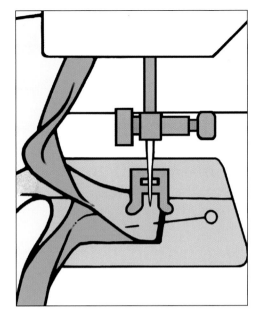

16. Fold the binding to the back side of the quilt. Pin in place so that the folded edge on the binding covers the stitching line. Tuck in the excess fabric at each miter on the diagonal.

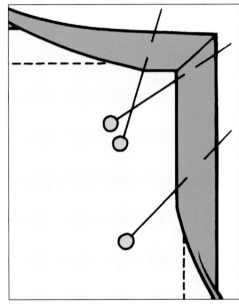

17. From the right side, "stitch in the ditch" using invisible thread on the front side, and a bobbin thread to match the binding on the back side. Catch the folded edge of the binding on the back side with the stitching.

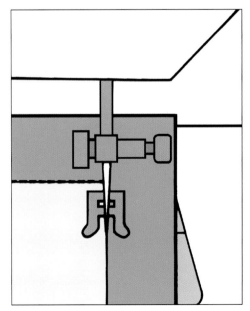

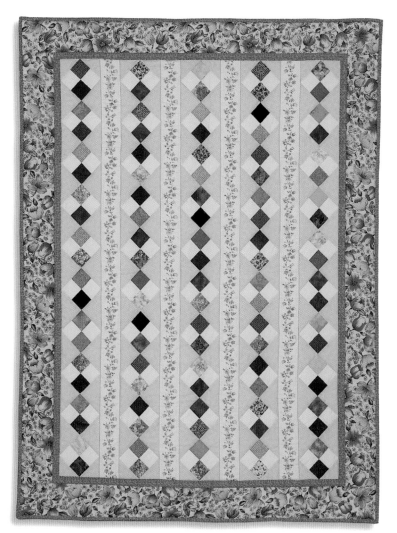

Teresa Varnes   49" x 66"

Bonus Four Patch Quilt

This is a scrappy, build-as-you-go type of quilt using any leftovers you may have from your Small Block Quilt. These "leftover quilts" often become your favorites! Make the Four Patches using the excess fabric from your layered strips, or from 2½" strips.

Teresa used all the Four Patches left over from her Small Block Twin sized Double Pinwheel quilt and turned them into a lap robe size Four Patch Quilt. You can make a smaller wall-hanging using this same technique.

For each Vertical Strip, you need:		
Half Square Triangles	(1) 3¾" square for each end Cut in half on one diagonal	◩
Quarter Square Triangle	(1) 7" square for every 2 Four-Patches Cut in fourths on both diagonals	⊠
Dividing Strips	3½" wide by length of vertical strip	

1. Assembly-line sew your Four-Patches together.

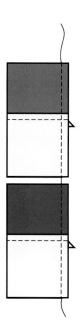

2. For each vertical Four Patch strip, lay out a unit for each end from two half square triangles, and one quarter square triangle.

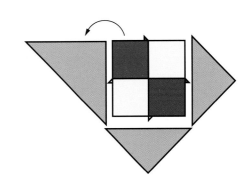

3. Flip Four-Patch to quarter square triangle. Match up straight tops. Let tip hang over at bottom. Sew, and press seam toward triangle.

4. Center half square triangle on Four Patch. Flip right sides together. Match tip of triangle to center seam of Four Patch. Sew, and press seam toward triangle.

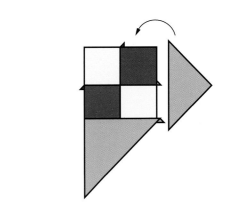

5. Center half square triangle on Four Patch. Flip right sides together. Sew, and press seam toward triangle.

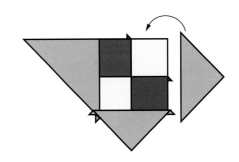

6. Assembly-line sew quarter square triangles to remaining Four Patches.

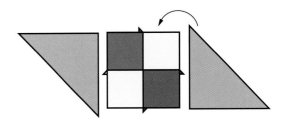

7. Press seams toward triangles. Trim tips.

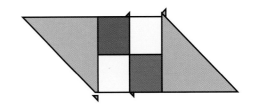

8. Lay out pieces, and sew together into vertical rows. Lock seams on Four Patches.

9. Trim edges even, maintaining ¼" seam allowance.

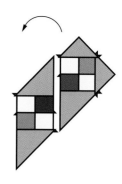

10. Alternating Four Patch strips and stripes, pin and sew vertical rows together.

11. Frame the quilt top with a 1½" framing border.

12. Add a 5" border.

13. Quilt and bind.

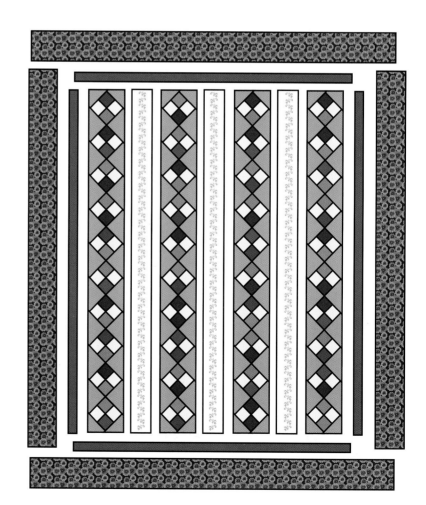

Quilted Travel Bag

This is the perfect project for using left over Small blocks, or start from the beginning and make new blocks for this easy project. You need sixteen Small Blocks and eight Small Half Blocks.

Designed by Luckie Yasukochi

Left Over Small Blocks

Identical

16 Small Blocks

8 Half Blocks

or

Mirror Image

8 Quilt Small Blocks

4 Quilt Small Half Blocks

8 Border Small Blocks

4 Border Small Half Blocks

New Three Fabric Small Blocks

    (10) 2½" Background strips
    (5) 2½" Medium strips
    (5) 2½" Dark strips

Additional Materials

(2) 12" sports zippers
1⅛ yds lining fabric
45" x 45" lightweight cotton batting
Ultra Suede, Heavy Corduroy, or Denim
    (2) 4" x 44" for Handles
    (1) 7" x 21" for Bottom
    (1) 7" x 21" Heavy weight interfacing
    (1) 7" x 21" cotton batting

Making the Blocks

1. Use left over blocks, or make a total of 16 Small Blocks and 8 Small Half Blocks.

2. Sew blocks together.

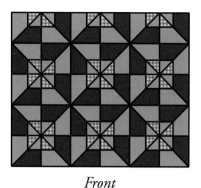

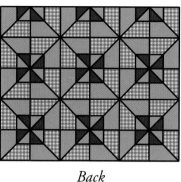
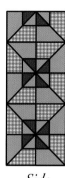

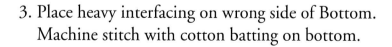

Front   *Side*   *Back*   *Side*

3. Layer each piece right side up with cotton batting and machine quilt through all layers. Trim batting to edge of quilt. Zigzag raw edges together.

4. Measure each piece and cut four lining pieces the same size. Cut a lining piece 7" x 21" for Bottom. Cut optional pockets and stitch in place.

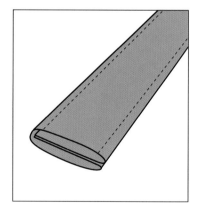

Handles and Bottom

1. **Handles:** Press in half wrong sides together. Open, and press again. Edge stitch both sides.

2. Pin Handles in place on front and back, and edge stitch. Stitch across at the Half Block.

3. Place heavy interfacing on wrong side of Bottom. Machine stitch with cotton batting on bottom.

Bottom   *Assembled Bag with Handle*

Lining the Bag

1. Sew four quilted pieces together. Sew ends together.

2. Insert Bottom, matching corners. Pin and sew. Leave quilted bag inside out.

3. Sew lining pieces together. Insert lining bottom. Turn right side out.

4. Place quilted bag inside lining bag, wrong sides together.

5. Pin top edges together and zigzag.

6. Pinch top edges together. Sew in 4" on both sides with ½" seam allowance. Trim.

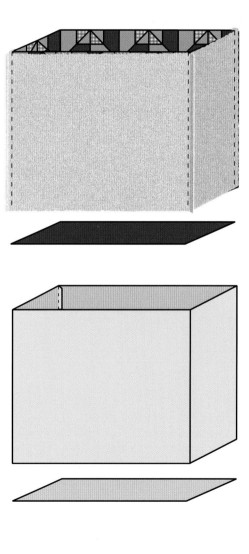

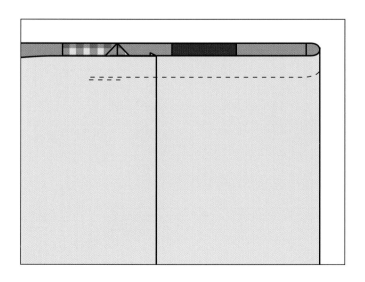

Inserting the Zippers

1. Turn right side out.

2. Baste under ½" seam allowance on each side.

3. Open zippers.

4. Fold back ends of zippers. Beginning with the ends in the middle, pin zippers into seam allowance. Make sure teeth are on folded edge.

5. Stitch in place. Hand tack ends.

6. Tack down corners from right side. Sew buttons at tacked corners.

Index

Acknowledgements

Special thanks to the quiltmakers:
Bobbie Ball, Sue Bouchard, Linda Fornaca, Marty Halus, Peggy Kile, Trish Kuncewicz,
Julia Markovitz, Laura McCauley, Vivien McNeece, Aiko Rogers, Urbana Schneider, Loretta Smith,
Shirley Stegmuller, Teresa Varnes, and Luckie Yasukochi.

Order Information

Quilt in a Day books offer a wide range of techniques and are directed toward a variety of skill levels.
If you do not have a quilt shop in your area, you may write or call for a complete catalog and current
price list of all books and patterns published by Quilt in a Day®, Inc.

Quilt in a Day®, Inc. • 1955 Diamond Street • San Marcos, CA 92069
1 800 777-4852 • Fax: (760) 591-4424 • www.quilt-in-a-day.com

Anniversary Florals

by Eleanor Burns

Multi-fabrics: Anniversary Florals and Benartex Companion prints

Many of the Double Pinwheel quilts were made with Anniversary Florals by Eleanor Burns for Benartex, Inc. The cover quilt also features many of the Anniversary Florals and Benartex companion prints. If you would like to recreate the examples, ask for these fabrics by name at your local quilt shop.

BENARTEX COLLECTION INTERNATIONAL

Two Fabric Quilt:
#246 Flower Puffs, Blue
#243 Forget-Me-Nots, Blue

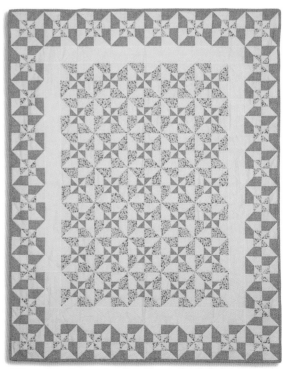

Three Fabric Quilt:
##243 Forget-Me-Nots, Yellow & Blue
#240 Flower Basket, Light Blue
#241 Eleanor's Lace